hope
to carry on

Knowing God's comfort in life and death

When somebody close to you dies, it can feel as if your world has fallen apart.

Times like these make us ask big questions: Why did this happen? What will life be like now? How will I cope? How will I carry on without them?

Even if we weren't close to them, the death of a friend, colleague or neighbour often leaves us thinking about our own mortality, and wondering what this short life of ours is about – and what happens next? Maybe you're worried about your own death.

This little booklet is to encourage and help you. It explains what God has done so that we can have comfort in the face of death. It will show how you can be sure that death is not the end, and how you can have real hope – both now and for the future.

Let's begin by considering some comforting words from God's word, the Bible. They describe a time when all the things that spoil our lives and the world now will be completely done away with, and when God will make everything new:

> *"He will wipe every tear from their eyes. There will be no more death or mourning or crying or pain, for the old order of things has passed away." He who was seated on the throne said, "I am making everything new."*
>
> The Bible: Revelation chapter 21 verses 4-5

It sounds wonderful, doesn't it? We like new things but we also know how new things eventually become old, spoiled or worn out.

It's a bit like us. At birth, we are new and appear unspoiled. But with time we grow up, and then grow old, and our lives are spoiled in all kinds of ways – by unkindness, our own foolishness, broken relationships, sickness, grief, and in the end, by death.

But God has promised that one day he will make *everything new*. God's new world will be a place without crying or death or pain; without hospitals or hearses. We can't fully imagine how brilliant it will be because crying, pain, and death so often spoil our lives.

People say that death is part of life – and it is. But we hate it. There is a reason for that: we were not made for death – we were made for life. The Bible says:

> *God has made everything beautiful in its time. He has also set eternity in the human heart…*
>
> The Bible: Ecclesiastes chapter 3 verse 11

That's how God made us – he made us for eternity. He made us to live. Death is the opposite of what we were designed for. And we feel it very deeply – both when a loved one dies, and in the fact that no one wants to die.

That's why we try to keep healthy: some of us cut down on smoking or drinking, others do exercise – and some people even eat salad! And as we do those things we reflect how God made us… for life… with eternity in our hearts. *So why do we die?*

Why death?

Many people wonder *"Why?"* – Why do we have to die? Why does death have to spoil life?

God made us and loves us. But although he loves us, the fact is, left to ourselves, we don't love him as we should.

We live as if God is not there. We live in his world, and enjoy all that he has made, but we ignore him… or only call on him when we want something. The Bible calls this "sin".

Ignoring God like this means that we are cut off from

him. We are like a bunch of cut flowers: we look alive and well, but as we all know, cut flowers are actually dead flowers. They are dead because they are cut off from their roots – from the source of life.

Being cut off from God (through our sin) is to be cut off from the ultimate source of life – and that is why, like cut flowers, we all die. The Bible puts it like this:

For the wages of sin is death…

Although people's lives may end through no particular fault of their own (illness, accidents, war, etc.), the Bible says that ultimately we all die because we all reject God – the giver of life – and try to live our lives without him.

This is God's fair and right judgment on all human beings. But because he programmed us for life, we naturally hate death. It goes against all our instincts. But there is help and there is hope…

Why Jesus?

1 *Jesus died on a cross*
Despite being rightly angry with us because of our sin, God loved the world so much that he sent his Son, Jesus, to save us. Although Jesus was born as a man, he was different. He did not ignore God. He was not cut off from God. He did not deserve to die.

But he did die. And it's brilliant news for us that he did! It is through his death that people like us can be forgiven and receive the God-given longing of our hearts – eternal life. The Bible verse on the previous page continues like this:

> *For the wages of sin is death, but the free gift of God is eternal life in Christ Jesus our Lord.*
>
> The Bible: Romans chapter 6 verse 23

People think that their own death takes them to be with God. It doesn't. It is Jesus' death that makes it possible for us to be right with God and, one day, to be with him for ever.

But how?

The apostle Peter wrote:

Christ ... died for sins once for all; the righteous for the unrighteous, to bring you to God.

The Bible: 1 Peter chapter 3 verse 18

Although Jesus was perfectly right with God ("righteous"), he died. He died to pay the price of sin for people like us, who are not right with God ("unrighteous"). His purpose was to bring us to God. Through his death we can be forgiven by God now, and ready to meet him when we die.

Wonderfully, neither the cross where Jesus died, nor our own death is the end…

2 Jesus rose from the dead

Jesus' death is a grim mark of this world, but his resurrection is a glimpse of what is available in the future to everyone who trusts him. It gives us hope – the hope to carry on – for it tells us very loudly and very clearly that *death is not the end*. Through the resurrection of Jesus, our great enemy, death, has been defeated. And this victory is not just for Jesus; it is for anyone who will believe in him. The apostle Paul wrote:

> *We know that the one who raised the Lord Jesus from the dead will also raise us.*
>
> The Bible: 2 Corinthians chapter 4 verse 14

Just as Jesus was raised from the dead, so one day, those who truly believe in him will also be raised to new life – ready for God's new creation, where suffering, decay, sin and death will be absent.

This is such great news! This is the Christian hope – not based on wishful thinking, but on the real, physical resurrection of Jesus. And the great thing is that we can have this new life too. It is life that can start today but go on beyond the grave, because Jesus offers it freely to everyone who will believe and trust in him.

3 *Jesus offers help, hope and life*
A Christian is someone who loves and trusts Jesus. They follow him as their Lord and Saviour. He said:

> *"I am the way and the truth and the life. No one comes to the Father except through me."*
>
> The Bible: John chapter 14 verse 6

Jesus is the way for people who are lost. If we want direction, we need Jesus. He is the only way to a right relationship with God, and the only way through death.

Jesus is also the truth for people who are confused. Experience tells us that we can't totally trust anyone – even those closest to us can let us down. But Jesus is the truth: he is the one person who can be totally relied on – and especially in the face of bereavement and death. He even rose from the dead – just as he said he would!

Finally, Jesus is the life. He has the answer to death – and proved it by rising from the dead! Most of us are scared of death. But Jesus has taken on death and won. That's why he is able to get *us* through death and give us the eternal life we crave. And we do crave it – which is why almost no one wants to die. We need Jesus – more than we need anyone or anything. He says: "No one comes to the Father except through me."

Those who do come to Jesus become God's children. They have a heavenly Father, who loves and cares for them and who is always with them – whatever troubles or griefs life may bring. Through Jesus, we have help and hope in life, but we also have help and hope in death.

If Jesus is the way, the truth and the life, then the thing to do is to believe and trust in him. If you would like to, you can express that belief and trust in Jesus by saying a simple prayer…

> *Lord God, you know what it is like to lose someone close to you.*
>
> *Thank you that you understand the grief and sorrow I am going through now.*
>
> *Thank you for sending Jesus into the world to die for us so that we can come back to you*
> > *and be forgiven.*
>
> *Thank you that Jesus rose again to give me new life and hope and comfort in the face of death.*
>
> *Please help me to trust Jesus as the way, the truth and the life.*
>
> > > > *Amen.*

What now?

You may have many questions about what it means to be a Christian. Ask the person who gave you this booklet for help. Or you could visit **www.christianityexplored.org** to discover more about what it means to follow Jesus.

God answers our prayers, and he promises to come close to those who come close to him. As you trust Jesus, God will come to live in you by his Holy Spirit, and help you to live as one of God's children.

The local church is the place where you will meet other members of God's family. Christian faith is personal, but it is never private. It is as a member of the local church that you will be encouraged and helped to grow as a Christian. We all need help and encouragement – that's why God has given us to each other. To find a church near you, see **www.findachurch.org.uk**

Why does death spoil our lives?
Is there any hope?
How can we be sure that there
is life beyond the grave?

This booklet answers these big questions
so that you can know personally good
comfort in life and death.

FAITH MISSION
£ 1.20

thegoodbook
COMPANY

thegoodbook.com | co.uk

ISBN 978-1-90955-904-2

9 781909 559042

Christian Life / Bereavement

Hope to carry on:
Knowing God's comfort in life and death
© Pete Jackson/The Good Book
Company, 2013. Reprinted 2017, 2018.

Bible quotations taken from The Holy
Bible, New International Version, NIV
Copyright © 1973, 1978, 1984, 2011 by
Biblica, Inc. Used by permission. All
rights reserved worldwide.

Design by André Parker
ISBN: 9781909559042 | Printed in the UK

the**good**book
COMPANY

Published by The Good Book Company
Tel (UK): 0333 123 0880
International: +44 (0) 208 942 0880
Email: info@thegoodbook.co.uk

Websites:
UK: www.thegoodbook.co.uk
North America: www.thegoodbook.com
Australia: www.thegoodbook.com.au
New Zealand: www.thegoodbook.co.nz